A False Nanny

Anna Krushelnitskaya

Copyright © 2021 by Anna Krushelnitskaya
All Rights Reserved
ISBN: 978-1-64180-120-1

Cover art by Margaret Romano-Krushelnitskaya

Published by
Front Edge Publishing
42807 Ford Road, Canton, MI

HAND

I've lived a long life
With my hand in my pocket
I do everything
With my other hand
One hand is real handy
One hand in my pocket
Awaits reattachment
Though chances are slim

THEN

Tomorrow morning, I was hit with time,
Had to dismount and sit in Winchell Park,
A temporary structure in my mouth,
What dentists call a cantilever bridge,

The sandbox temporarily removed,
The past where all the punctuation lives
Upon a time; upon a plastic horse,
I saw my baby rocking back and forth.

"Do you like Kipling?" as the question goes.
"Don't know, I've never kippled!" goes the quip.
I think I've kippled, kippled! Time performed
A double-rejet enjambment. Somersaults,

A cantilever bridge of IF and THEN.
(And treat those two impostors just the same
To serve your turn long after they are gone,
Then you will know how selfish people are.)

I sat there and I just could not believe
How firm it was, and heavy under me.
New babies dotted space, all ready for
The park. I rocked myself a little loose.

New stroller babies strained. Masked strangers strolled.
The anesthesia started wearing off.
I breathed. I swallowed. I could feel my nose.
I got into my spacesuit and drove home.

NURSERY RHYMES

Anna Wanna, let's take a look now,
Higgledy-piggledy, do not disturb,
Anna Wanna, she made a book now.
This is the book, and this is its blurb.
Higgledy-piggledy, hellicans-pelicans,
Holy-moly, half of it rhyme!
Doesn't she know that
No real Americans,
No real Americans
Read any rhyme?!
Spoonity-moonity, metric jejunity!
Better not show the poetics community.

ROOKS

You flew up and you said: I was once so, so sad; how can I never be sad again? I had this diagrammed, and then after that had it glued from beginning to end.

Yes, for me special questions are best, but I'll warn that today I'm not smiles, I am gripes, for my son was returned home for being too warm and there's howling again in the pipes.

Yes, just step on the scale, the brake, a rake; on the pain scale, gentle or rough? There's no glue to make sense of the things that break, we're just naming the broken stuff.

Yes, you can take a tour where it all exists, it just sits, it just is, sweet home sweet: yogurt cups, Scottish moors and Pacific mists, and left turns, and rooks in the wheat.

Yes, you did many tries, as reflected in chart, to do something as well as to be, with your tunnel eyes and your narrow heart and one clogged valve that pumps just for me.

Yes, I was ten times three, I walked into a tree predicated on being as glue: to be what makes sense, to be free to be free, to be long, deep and close with a few.

Yes, the question was "Now what?" and both "Nothing!" and "I-love-you!" were true enough; a forget-me-not, no-can-do-anything, and i-love-you is just naming stuff.

Yes, we can take a tour where it all exists, take a look, take a day, play a game, maybe we can stay out till it's ten times six, see how many rooks we can name.

Yes, we are getting stuck, but also unglued, gotta make sure we're lodged for the night, yes, I'm getting annoyed, yes, I am getting short, every day, both in temper and height.

Yes, please step off the scale, the brake, the rake; on the scale, where are you, one to ten? I normally write down the pulse that I take, just forgot what the question was then.

Rakes are stacked in the shed, time is spooled in the watch, rooks are strewn in good disharmony; I'm a cobbler unshod, just don't die while I watch, and perhaps don't ask so much of me.

RAMPART

I forgot all the big mystical events in my life.
Their halos died.
Things I wish for: contiguous library shelves labeled *writers I agree with* and *books for sad people*.
But I'm afraid sad people gathering near the implicating shelf would be accosted by well-meaning citizenry with popcorn, either force-fed or from a slingshot.
That syntax was intentionally iffy.
I would also like a library shelf marked *intentionally iffy granma*.
Perchance the iffy shelf would shield the sad shelf people from well-meant popcorn; serve as a great undercover neuro antipopcorn rampart.

WORDSMITH

I wandered, lonely and a clown,
And no one thought too much of me.
My funny face was often found
In jerk-and-joker company.
I didn't sport too many frills.
I didn't fit too many bills.

How often on my couch I lie
In lonely or in pensive mood.
To walls I cast a rollward eye,
And, back at me, the walls are rude.
I thought – I thought – but little luck.
I'm stupid and a daffy duck.

HOLE

All my cogitation holes are big.
My children know mama does not answer short, simple and wrong.
Mama must explain the whole thing.
I am in a cogitation hole getting ready for my father to die again.
I've sat in this one for thirty-six hours.
Since I began writing this sentence it's really only been twenty-four, but I know that by the time I take a nap break in the hole it will have been an intermediate thirty-six and counting, and I do not know when I am due to emerge.
I have to be silently intimate with many things. It is like drawing the map of a galaxy where a new star only becomes visible after you've mapped its nearest neighbor, and then you put it on, and then the one to the left, to the top, to the wing, to the Earth's southwest lights up.
It is like blood flooding and stretching the sleeves of a prepared cellophane structure, first the points nearest the entry, then mid- and distant points and branches, the abstract blue blood from a tampon commercial, blood from the aneurism floods my father's brain, his blood pressure skyrockets, he is already down but the ambulance has not picked him up yet from the hedge by the supermarket.
The more perturbed, the less communicative, like father like me, I attend to my daily tasks like a pro flyswatter with a fly swatter: with automaticity and zero investment.
My real day job is in the hole and it is not complete until I've built the thing, walked into it and lit a match.
Like head cheese, it is a dish long-cooking; brains, brains, pacing and mumbling.
My father is now in the hospital where no one knows him, and no one knows he is there.
I was not provided exposure or description, so I have to cogitate his experience, fear, pain, expiration, the more perturbed the more silent, while the public around me ask the inane question of if I'm okay, read short and wrong things off some da zi bao, shout them into the air dense with the current signifiers of currency.
Don't yell around the cogitation hole. You will cause a landslide and I will need to map the can of hooch in my father's limp hand all over again.

03/04/1945 – 02/07/2018

I don't want to go to your poisonous shore
I hear war is raging you're hiding a scam
I was not informed of what people you are
Ill-formed hurtful spiky and not very sane

At sea in the sea with my wet merrymen
I don't want to go to your poisonous shore
The stain on your dress is shaped like a squid
The chain on the anchor the chain of events

Adrift in my chair with some booze by my foot
A rift in my map it was not a good map
I don't want to go to your poisonous shore
The store the post office but that will be that

Pin me down to the deck pour some rum down the plank
Stretch me out on a bed zip me tight in a bag
I'm flotsam I'm jetsam in this freezing gown
I don't want to go to your poisonous shore

KITCHEN

a fly a fly
a flyspeck a fly
a flyspeck a fly a flyspeck a fly
a flyspeck a flyspeck a flyspeck a fly
a fly a fly
a flyspeck a fly

HANDOUT

A handy compendium of introductory tedium.

By Hemingway: I was born. I sat in a social medium.

By John Irving: On the day of their dark and stormy June wedding my parents received word that my father's brother had killed himself. Twenty-five years would pass between that day and another June afternoon when a strange male Great Dane, by some dog imperative, ran up to me as I sat on a pebbly Siberian riverbank and pissed all over my long pleated polyester skirt. Only seventeen years would pass between the wedding June and the June afternoon when a strange slit-eyed sweaty dipshit wearing speedos, by some dog imperative, sauntered out of the thin Russian olives lining up another pebbly Siberian riverbank and petted my naked shoulder, his palm wet and gluey with fresh sperm.

LINNAEUS

I'll apply to you with a lonely appeal on my fucking flying banana peel; with my blood pressure dropping my call will land on the sharp outcropping on which you stand with your muscles, your khakis, your helmet of pith, with your misty eyes an all-distant myth, with your boots that are tall and your stance that is wide, to have my petition seen and denied.

If there might be a way to you, then it is through progressively smaller entities, by appealing to love me and to understand to a spider, a spore, to a grain of sand, through the underlings and the preliminaries, until one of them, the smallest there is, approves my filing and stamps it, and then I can take it up to the spiders again,

And in tedium up the Linnaean myriad, each with a different waiting period, each with a different color seal, each will perhaps escalate my appeal up where your soul sits in deflecting vapors, to contend by the show of my inks and my papers I might be, at least in the spiders' esteem, somewhat worthy of love and humane honesty.

SQUARE

I have to fight dirty
I cannot win square
Fingernails in eye sockets
Teeth in the carotid

Sending wan smiles
To your friend Dipshit Van Winkle
To wake him up to the option
Of saving me for himself

I can shake him off later
With a promise of sometime later
But I can't shake off your boulder fist
Once it lands and ruptures my spleen

SOVIET OBSTETRICS

If the trends keep
By 2022
The cheerfulness and tact
I project
Will match those contained
In a 1932
Soviet textbook
For obstetric nurses.

KAI'S EYES

The wind bitch-slaps him. He rubs his burning eyes.
He sees the new world and he tries it on for size.

It's small and ugly. His hands are cold. Hard to breathe.
The sky's a dead dome above and the earth underneath.

Such a nasty rose! It's a vulva, it's maggot food.
Children peck at his woolen coat – what a clueless brood.

Like shiny-eyed finches, they play in the grey, in the brown.
What's a boy to do on the day his blood slows down?

He can't smile, he can't spend a dime, he can't give a damn
For constructing this irredeemable pentagram.

Children flock away cheerfully chirping: he's very strange.
No-one wants his report from the bottom of the cage.

A QUATRAIN ON WHY YOUTH IS EXHAUSTING

Young people don't sleep because they're concerned with concerns that happen at night.
They don't know what they are talking about; they don't know it and talk all the time.
Forever they look in the mirror to see someone interesting there, yet they don't.
Someone tells them I-love-you-I-don't-love-you – it's the friggin' news of the year.

E2E4

September, we return from summer
As fattened calves
Previously known as have-nots
And newly haves
Eyepaint the color of wisteria
Depeche Mode perms
We meet by the Café Siberia
On unknown terms
E2E4 your terms are scarier
You smoke so well
Your pack of smokes is from Bulgaria
My mouth is hell
Your name is Anya mine is Anya
Thing One Thing Two
You have a sidewalk-length dress on ya
I'll sew one too
You move your knight, swear like a sailor
You've kissed with tongue
I am a child a teenage failure
I am a pawn
I move a grade up on the first day
Next to a queen
First of July it was your birthday
I've never been

ANURA

If you tell them you will kill me, if you burn it you will burn me, if you strip me you will sell me down the river, down the Styx. Please just keep this to yourself and you will keep me to yourself; but I can see it in your fool eyes you are thinking of a fix. I can see you febrile siblings hacking over bready brew and I can see their slit-eyed wives serve turnips garnished with fresh dirt! I stretch my small skin on a rack and that just lets me be with you because this small and bumpy frog skin, silly, that's my only shirt.

All my gowns are ghosts and gauze – have you thought of my life before you? No, you haven't: you're a fool. You just feel smug: you got a wife. I'm your first success with women, I am paddling, an amphibian, I'm just clinging to the living, I'm just clinging to a life. You dimly took me in your hands and of my name did not inquire; it's Vasilisa Svet Anura, which means *she without a tail*. Do you really think it was you who I dreamed of in that mire? Let me tell you how it ends, the only friend in my avail.

I can't fake human anymore if you have my frog skin burned, if you have my frog skin ground and stretched and torn and ripped and burned; I'll thwack myself against the floor, my brain will buzz, my spine will hurt, but I will have to hit the ground and I will have to be a bird. Fire safety regulations: keep my skin away from fire! You remind me of the Firebird: see the blaze but think of grain. Interdiction violations: what do you think will transpire? You remind me of the Firebird: you are also that bird-brained.

Yes, I am in a shit vessel, only one I am allowed. I can be a frog with you, or I can be a bird and gone. You might briefly see my essence: turquoise smoke in steely clouds. It will be forty times beyond you when it's Forty Lands Beyond. Then, your family will lie: the fool did save his animal bride, scouting bravely hill and dale and all the Forty Lands across, weft and warp! And I'll just fly, a homeless hopeless lonely flatheart. I'll gain wings, I'll gain a tail, I'll gain the voice to sing the lost.

ROUND ROBIN

On the corner of several Life Avenues,
I was courted by Knowledge
And maybe by Fame.
I was doing quite well at that blind interview.
My bluestockings checked out.
My credentials, same.

We sat and we nodded Chicago-style.
I was having a coffee
And a Paris-Brest.
Then I looked out the window where Love walked by,
A marvelous beast
With a checkered chest.

I took a big bite
Of the cream and the choux,
Left a hurried and generous tip on the check,
Then I walked through the doors on some Life Avenue,
And I buried my face
In Love's unbuttoned neck,

Rolled-up sleeves of warm sinew
And buffalo check.
Love took out a flask and poured me a drink.
I forgot that something was something I knew.
Love and I had a litter of pellets, I think.

I misplaced my credentials and changed my name.
My bluestockings tore and the wind was hard.
Unchaste, I walked chased
By the whistling of Shame
Down 44th Sunset Boulevard.

Then, a rifle from Chekhov,
In one tiny tap,
Left a checkmark, a checkmate on my red breast,
And the wind stole and tossed
My white dunce cap
For taking and failing
The marshmallow test.

BRIDE

You open yourself like a fridge
And out of you comes a bride
In a music box chiming with extras
And a lipsticked mother-in-law

A mother-in-law plays a role
A bride is made of a mission
A groom can be made of a mission
Or can simply play a role

A bride is a white hopeful heart
A bride's mission, to kiss the world whole
A sturdy bride can be reused
A freak bride can be used five times

Your bride smokes a cigarette
She giggles and kisses with tongue
The cigarette smoke seeps through
The ruptures too big for a kiss

You close yourself like a fridge
And in to die goes the bride
Against her early belief
The bride never married no-one

GRAINS OF WRATH

I'll water my vodka plantation
At three a.m. in the yard
This woman is thirsty
This lawn is thirsty
It needs my attention
Stat
You're only thirteen my daughter
Why did you wake up at three
This lawn needs water
This woman needs water
Hard water I said
Go to sleep
I was just out with some friends now
I was only out with some friends
I'm back from out with some friends now
Just ladies
Go back to bed
There's a gash in my thigh from shaving
Except it is not on my thigh
Except it is not from shaving
I just fell a bit
Go to sleep
I'll harvest my vodka harvest
I call it my grains of wrath
You're only thirteen
God she's only thirteen
Oh my God when is this gonna end

FINE

Prisons are full of somebody's children
Rehabs are full of somebody's children
Graveyards are full of somebody's children
Stop fucking saying she'll be fine it's a phase
Booze gets manufactured
Coke gets manufactured
Meth gets manufactured
They need to go in someone
The Church of All-Stupid-Ass-Beliefs
Has packets of brain insect eggs
They need to go in someone
Nothing personal
It's just your children's numbers were called
They need to go

OMAHA STAKES

Omaha, you sleep in your boyfriend's shirt.
New York, you sleep in your girlfriend's bra.
So you tap yourself on the back
To pat yourself on the back:
Tap-tap-tap-up-up-up-up-up-up-pat-pat-pat,
Good job New York, good job Omaha.

You arrived at my door in an egg of mess
(Bullets, pellets, nickels, erythrocytes)
Told me not to call 911,
Said the shell and the contents were mine,
You were drunk, you were high, you were sick, you were nuts,
You were nuts, psychopaths, megatons, terabytes.

California carried Nixon and Bush.
California wanted to live alone.
Reagan wore a hat and said hi.
London wore a hat and said hi.
You said me, you said I, you said west, you said coast.
I sat waiting silently cooking a stone.

To be young today in this land is to sleep.
To be young today in this land is to thrash.
Screamers signing the Bill of Goods,
Dreams and memories needing meds.
You said I really am, you were shrapnel sharp,
I said please be a peaceful friend to your flesh.

There's an old tired tapestry over my bed.
It is hanging skewed and threadbare and skirled.
No it's not the end of the world,
But what is the end of the world?
The end of the world, the end of the world,
The end of the world is the end of the world.

PROG

I live in five-minute increments
I step on a measuring tape
Yellow safety tape measuring tape
I step through five-minute binary gates
Inside/outside: outside shoes
Laces/no laces: no laces
Laces lead to slips strips and sprawls
Dumpster/recycling: dumpster
Inside/outside: inside shoes
Child/no child: child
Lunchtime/not lunchtime: lunch
Own lunch/ child's lunch: child
Child's what/ nothing: what
Sorry bad battery
Energy/no energy: no energy
Nap/wine: wine
Lunchtime/ not lunchtime: lunch
Own lunch/wine: wine
Own lunch/child's lunch: child
Protein carb fiber hydration plate
Serving serves shoots and leaves
Oversee consumption/ not: not
Work/not work: work
Project 1/ Project 2/ Project 3/ Project 4/ Project 5: what
Sorry bad battery
Wine/ nap: nap
End of day/ start of day: end
Hold onto stair rails when descending
To be safe from steps slips and spins
Right hand/ left hand: right

Right hand/ left hand: left
2 a.m. pee/ not pee: not
2 a.m. starless arresting death
Endure/ not endure: endure

HARDBOILED

And then there was that one time I was all hardboiled
I leaned in a sheriffal pose up the whole Wyoming
My gun drilled a dip in the sand with its non-business end
I spat out three rare-earth words with their tips chewed off

Then I went on a trip of power to the Great Gator Isles
My minions scattered like rats from my platinum heel
My mwah-ha-ha-money flowed through my offshore accounts
Dead bodies were buried and nobody issued a squeak

And then there was that one time I was voted most loved
All beauty contests shut down in bankrupt shame
Asleep on a blanket of sable my golden orbs heaved
All men danced around me and I didn't work a day

Then I went cratering everybody's blessed peace
I fell and I needed a village to raise me from need
I fell again and the village picked up their phones
In dread of the trills in my vulnerable voice

DOGGO

Mama! A man with a suitcase followed me home!
Can I keep him? Ohno. Need to make a decision quickly.
Looks like one of those messes only contained by a wife.
He will slosh in the wife and make her unstable and sickly.
Sweet darling, it looks like you are on a poorly planned run
Out the wife, so I won't take you in and I ask you to please be
Understanding: I'll have to keep you in the park long enough
To toss you a frisbee, a frisbee, a frisbee, a frisbee…

COTILLION

If you have time come see me in the night
Where I am a rebellion
A gentle carillon
Unknown
A feather
In my true state
Asleep against the world
In your true state
A feather
Afloat
A friendly gentleman
Affray in a cotillion
What are the chances you could spare a dance

RABBIT HAT

Tell you about myself?

Ancient History, Modern History or Breaking News?

I'm recovering from a cold, my eyeballs roughed up with sandpaper and my epiglottis with a metal file, and I wouldn't mind a nap with a friend, to be honest with you, which I selectively and startlingly will be now.

I was known as a bar wit and pickpocket bar excellence, bar none, and although now I am past my prime, I am past legalities, I want to skip the verification and go straight to the monkey business of bars, to palmistry, phrenology, grooming, drinking and the study of the iris.

Don't know why you would insist on verification at your age, you are no spring monkey yourself, but okay, suppose breeding will out, so here goes: I am a human female, my parents were ghonest burghers of Ghent but now they are ghost burghlars of Pittsburgh because, as you know, that's the only Ameriburgh allowed to keep its H.

Wanna hear a joke? Two of us walk into a bar. How many bulbs does it change to take light? Two, but you got'em both: presto change-o! You are prime company, and other people are too many.

That was Breaking News.

In Ancient History, I was a bulb.

In Modern History, I was unexpectedly prime rib, and I knew Adam from Adam, but that's sliding off now in a puddle of wrinkled snakeskin around my ankles, thank you everyone who was able to attend.

In the special skills section of my resume, I am a ticker tape that's too fast for your eyeballs, you catch every fifth word, and they add to prime iambic pentameter, indivisible, addictive and wrong under God; I am a bullet train from no-one to wife, but the tickets are never for sale. Rabbit! Hat! Cape! Scalpel! I see the pain in your eyes, dear. See my hand on your kneecap? My interrupted lovecord-line-cordyline follows the central ridge of your corduroy but we cannot verify that because of the full inversion of the palm. Alcohol! Gauze! You are my newest and best friend.

Unfortunately, our buzzer just went off.

DEFAULT

I've never defaulted on anything
Never been undefined – why?
I should turn out to be fun, right?
It should turn out fine

I got used to everything locally
This Tudor that seems haunted
This autumn that takes forever
The fruit of Korean dogwood

Both the prairie style and the prairie
A prairie would be pretty nice now
A couch&lambrusca prescription
An enterry in your diary

What do you mean – never?
How do I even get used to that
When faces fade in the upholstery
But I never forget voices?

Do you know how many balls I've dropped
Do you know how many charges
Do you know about that white hat that one time?
I can't tell you, you won't get to know me

Did you ever get hitched, stitched with anyone
Bellybutton to bellybutton
How often do you think we've all been duped
Did you have enough brain to think with?

Why is not everyone in a vat of booze
Not all music a bellyache of the blues
Alone we belly alone we ache
I know how to work a blueberry rake

Can I lie face-up in the blueberries
Unformed defaulted and formless
While your signature voice bubbles up in me
And sings like a mad Chinese thermos

SPLINTER

I've actually always wanted
To extract a splinter from you
I'm pretty crafty with splinters
That's what everybody says
I pity everyone differently
And you not more than the others
But the splinter's about you only
Or a bandage, that would also work
A splinter goes in like a needle
And I go in with a needle
You know I am best with a needle
I don't really like to tweeze
My hands are warm do not worry
I won't even hurt you hardly
You know I am never a problem
That's what everybody says
There's pretty much nothing that I need
And many things that I don't need
For instance, please buy me nothing
And never take me for a walk
For instance, no need to cry now
Although I for sure do lie now
You have the face of a person
Who likes his bourbon a lot
So where do you keep your first aid kit
Your peroxide gloves and Band-Aids
Although it would seem we have nothing
To infect each other with
So give me your little paw now
Grit your teeth and look out the window
You smell like resins and diesel
You dry streptocide person you

CAT STEVENS

We can't stand where we can't stand and I can't lean in where you're sitting; you speak with Cat Stevens time stamps, I can spit stanzas in one spitting; I'm small but I'm close so I seem tall and you're tall for somebody high; time has us beat as we beat the time and the eye is a trick of the eye.

MARLBOROUGH

Today I read of a beautiful garden with fronds, a rotunda, a pond, whose masters were bent on safeguarding the view of the Marlborough Downs beyond. I think pretty much anything is made well by the Marlborough Downs beyond, hence I will complete every thought, every spell with the Marlborough Downs beyond, as in, I will go to a grocery shop and the Marlborough Downs beyond, as in, I will buy me a bag of gumdrops and the Marlborough Downs beyond, as in, why don't you shut your piehole and the Marlborough Downs beyond, and I'll never dissever my soul from the soul of the Marlborough Downs beyond.

INSTA

I want to kick everyone out
And order Chinese food
And open a screwtop bottle of wine
And play my guitar loudly
And louder and drunker
Till nine p.m.
And then call someone up
Someone less familiar
And less advisable
He'd come over
And spend the night
Be kicked out in the morning
In the morning
I make hangover ramen soup
With canned corn
Take a nap at noon
Tomorrow six p.m.
Everyone may return
I can't believe you call it a poem
Cackled I in my syphilitic 19th century mezzo
This is literally word doodles
Not even words
Ickles
Poetry is brocade
This is wide-ruled paper

RUNE

This is my room
My home so to say
This is my bed
Where I every day
Or rather night
Lie down
Face down
On a dream
Of you
My friend
My blanket is down
I'm a pig within
I lie down face down
Dream yourself to me
And with this note
I'm making a knock
On your mind
Re: you
My friend
This is my bed
A mattress like all
Where I have dreams
Some nights, not all
Not every night
Or rather day
Sometimes
Re: you
My friend
This is my rune
She's a bit outland

Had a dream last night
I'll send you a scan
I'll just click save
And send you a fax
It will come out blind
But the fact is the fact
A dream last night
A thrill last night
Again
Re: you
My friend

SOUL

Love you are very squirmy today
Marvin Gaye oh oh Marvin Gaye
Love you are very squirmy tonight
Barry White ooh ooh Barry White
Thoughts are natural weeds of the brain
You remain ooh ooh you remain
Squirmy heavy elusive and big
Great White Pig oh oh Great White Pig

SQUID

I love with a disembodied love:
No passion squid three-hearted with desire,
No fissured flapping heart valve dreaming of
A patch. I love you with a love resigned.

The starter love, the ender, the betweener
Are made of carbonation and a vessel:
While Play-Doh started as wallpaper cleaner,
A children's tune became that song, Horst Wessel.

I offer you a glass of still or later,
I offer you a choice not taken, which
I offer with a side of age-related
Advanced directives posted on the fridge.

We only have the time for feelings whose
Recipient considers them of use.

WEIGHT

I am not happy with how gravity works on me anymore.

When I am in bed, I find I must have lost stuffing and feathers, and if there were marbles holding me down, then I have lost many.

Things are not holding me down and I can't fall asleep unless well-held.

I rotate my body on the mattress like I'm spit-roasting it, to distribute gravity evenly. If I don't, my fetal position does not work for sleep because my top leg is forty percent lighter than the leg underneath. I need to expose it to more gravity every so often lest I float away.

I place big hopes on the weighted blanket I ordered, its glass marbles to replace the marbles lost over many years to stealthy leaks.

My down duvet is a false nanny ready to betray me to Long Lankin.

I don't have anyone to hold me down and, given my age, I won't again.

Maybe I need to run aground more, take the legs off the bed, move the bedroom to the first floor, sleep in a soil trench.

BLANKET

She said, "Here's how it works: we use this nifty scanner, then we 3D-print an item of the found residuals.
You might have enough for a blanket. Some can only afford a tissue, so we make them a tissue.
But first, a few questions. Do you still get your periods? Are you ever disgusted to see kissing individuals?
A mouth always too full of saliva – has that recently seemed to become an issue?

Notice a belly that won't go away? Didn't you used to be a prizewinning breeding sow, actually?
I'm sorry, I'm joking. I'm not neurostandard, so I have a non-standard sense of humor.
I'm learning on the job. I've come to meet people here whose complaints I can understand at best intellectually.
Like, how they are sad they won't ever again wake up to the smell of a sleeping newborn.

But I guess everyone has their own sense of sad, as well as their own laughter.
Anyway, the impressions. We source them from the edited memory grotto.
If we use early affections, they must come from people who never saw you again after,
Or, if they did, it was on a heavily filtered, reputationally hefty vanity photo.

It's best to use sources who aren't yet dead, but there's no risk of an upcoming live encounter.
Your love blanket might stop working, since live encounters do get the weave perforated.
While the love residue is scraped from people whose neural activity was somewhat about you,
Its distortions must remain stably favorable rather than be updated.

As new generations age, they'll provide more protected, easier, sturdier fantamemory foam
To make their fantasy blankets from, sew them, stuff them and line,
Since so much of their love life is known as "talking" and is done from home
By lovers who only ever meet, message, imagine, project and break up online.

People ask: how can you grasp something like my love history, which is so idiosyncratic?
They don't realize all love histories are made from the same exact elemental matter.
We all nurse our special bees in our special bonnets, special bats in the special attic,
But the birds and the bees, the bees and the bats are all fauna, all high-protein batter.

Which is not to say we can capture loves exactly by scanning, scraping and replicating:
Scans can turn out abbreviated, distorted, approximate, folded or creased.
Our replication process produces something that's more like that famous cave painting:
Crude, schematic, but still giving a good impression of the hunt and the beast.

The love blanket itself is both interface and content.
It is only thoughts and affect, but thoughts and affect made slightly, a teensy bit, solidified.
Like, published poetry is both interface and content
Given to users who then make the thoughts and affect unsolidified.

Some clients insist on the tech details of our image converting before, heh, converting.
That's fine. Here's the booklet. When new tech comes out, it's normal for people to feel a bit leery,
But let's think back to the old interfaces, like the TV. Nobody finds TV disconcerting,
Even though most users, I'd say, don't understand television, its inner workings or theory.

Images are age-old content which gets captured through ever-evolving technique.
We invent new gadgets but not new people; people still employ taste, smell, feel, hearing and sight.
Photography arrests images, particular, situational, possibly private, unique,
All through the common and commonly accessible properties of light.

Our business is fully legal. We make a helpful societal aid that more people will soon embrace.
Remember the lawsuit against the inventors of the scanscrape technology Otto Weltig and Inge Linz?
The court ruled the so-called residual affective stamp was not intellectual property but simply a trace.
Traces of feelings are not created but left behind; they're not paintings but fingerprints.

The new legal issue is, we must weed old cruelties out of the scans. Abuse can't be replicated; it must be fixed.
It is our company's promise to the public, to history, and to a couple watchdog organizations.
Our clients' love traces are all from the past, so impure; so far, our weeding results have been mixed,
But we are perfecting our process and tech to fully comply with these important regulations.

I expect my questions about your periods were not a huge mystery. You might have already cracked it.
Our love blankets perform best for aging clients like you, who are not – and I have to be blunt –
Interested in the whole wet business of sex or can even attract it.
The love blanket works best draped undisturbed over their newly and steadily cold front.

Of course, we won't use major relationships for scanscraping: too much contradictory detail.
We like them short and intense, like, someone who knew you only a little, but whom you made hurt, happy or horny.
A suitable scrape is that super-drunk boy at the school dance who said to you, for some reason in French, *je t'aime!*
For teachers, doctors and therapists, students' and patients' crushes trace great, though the legal cleaning gets thorny.

So, you are fifty-five. Once we scanscrape enough off you, we'll move on to layering and to matching.
While you wait for the scanner, please enjoy our complimentary herbal tea.
Oh! If a source had left you in an ugly way, the blanket may get a little bit scratchy.
For now, we offer a limited range of colors and a limited warranty.

When you go to sleep, put the love blanket checkered side down, and you should feel something slightly related to being held by a lover.
Put it striped side down and, funnily, something like being attractive will weakly radiate through."
The phone rang. She answered the call pertly: "Welcome to *Lover to Cover!* We love to help! What can we cover today for you?"

DAPHNE

I said: my appointed master
Am I painted by Mary Cassatt?
Hyacinth narcissus daphne
This spring is smothersome stuffy
It's just this fatigue, and my tongue
Tastes of metal, and soil, and of wrong
You said: the tale of the train is coming along
As the train is coming along.
I said: out of sheer lizardness
Can I please hazard this
Leap and plant myself flat free from struggle?
You said: when the vein in your temple under my lips
Will no longer flutter.
I said: of this spring infatuation
Am I due to die in succession?
You said: grow patient.
I said: sin Apollo.
You said: all poison.
I said: why can't it go quicker?
You said: you have a built-in ticker.
I said: when did it start to unravel
You said: the day I pressed my hand on your navel.
I said: will you at least grow through me
Will I taste your waters
Will they solve the copper tang on my tongue
Will we for a minute belong
You said: the tale of the train is coming along
As the train is coming along.

FAILING FORWARD: AN INTERVIEW

Business: "Describe a time when you were failing forward."
Poet: "Failing forward
Is an afterlife
That is a type of heavy clay
When all your kids are viciously insane
And everybody speaks in acronyms.
That's why you go grieving
By the pond not by the river,
Because the river
Makes you think of going by.
And to put off the thoughts,
You yearn for a touch of the living,
A meaningful warm hand along the vertebrae;
A temporary beaming
Of eyes that helps with falling
Asleep and dreaming
That afterlife is humus."
Business: "So, that was failing forward?"
Poet: "Did you need a coda?
Da capo
Al fine."
Business: "Do you have experience
In B2B solutions?"
Poet: "Only as a Hamlet."

I HAUNT THE DISCO CLUB

I died and something dully said
Air sparkle NPD
And now I never go to bed
A sleepless deportee

I died and now my wife moved in
She painted hallways blue
She doesn't even have a man
There's no one to fly through

Now she who lived with me for years
Who was considered mine
Put all my ledgers in the trash
She never cracked a spine

She sold my Technics from upstairs
My music room upstairs
Where I was having gay affairs
My music room affairs

And now I haunt the disco club
I spin I strobe I thread
And now I do not have a bed
I cannot go to bed

And now I am a sparkly ghost
I sparkle EDM
I am the most I've been, the most
And no one knows I am

IN MEMORIAM

What we remember
About the diseased
Is how he lied
Proactively
With brawn
Outrage
A lying
Lance
On the offence
A legalist
Drawn
To tactical umbrage
As a default stance

Are you ready to charge me with anything
Who are your expert witnesses
What is it that you think I did
A copy of your evidence
Hire a PI then
A hurt face
Walking out
Leaving
Silence
A carapace
No one
Could squish him
He lived in a novel
By John Grisham

Every time
People stopped asking
He walked
A winner among men
Unassailable
Silently basking
Counting his victory
Adding it to the fold
Another copper penny
Shining to him like gold
Amen

FOR RICK

It is heartbreaking
You have nothing
To read with
A weird single
Male raisin
In a wooden cabin
And reason
A whore of feelings
We have too little
Too late
Like the dim-witted
Lestrade
With no one
To hug you
Except Budweiser
And Bukowski
And you wanted
To write a humor novel
Together
In correspondence
We are so sorry
You better
Believe it
But you probably have nothing
Left to believe with
Let's hope the Space Queen
Comes in the guise of Willie
The Groundskeeper
From the Simpsons

Replete with tentacles
Of pleasure
Fulfilling
And funny

GRAVITY HILL

Let us make a business of oddities!
Let us bottle them, peddle the vials:
Disgusted Sex and Defied Gravities,
Groovy Graves and Confirmed Denials.

Then, we will, as new experts in kooky,
Ride our fortunes astride and abreast
Of the horns of Perceived Slight Cookies
Where our fortunes will finally rest.

Fine purveyors of whatthefuckana,
Which we daringly have been amassing,
We'll develop a name and an honor,
Quaintly labeled and slightly off-gassing.

Thrown around for a loop by a shuffling of hands,
Switching trains midstream the Rio Grande,
We'll be off to consult in exciting lands
Where they celebrate Thursday on Monday.

Solar lunatics sampling snake oil fine and crude,
We'll be asked to advise in the palace.
We'll dissemble our syntax and move there for good,
Often lonely and slightly off-balance.

SLEEVES

In the past, the world didn't used to have all these sleeves.
We lived in a shed, ate leaves with a shovel, wore leaves.
Then, they made houses with ashtrays, houses without,
Pig-faced people in the north, bird-faced in the south,
Who split into women with cigarettes, women without,
Women with cigarettes in and out of the mouth,
Filterless, filtered, everything splits and splits,
Phobos, Deimos, two Mounds, two Almond Joys, Twix!
She rolls up the world in a mat and tucks in the ends,
She puts kitchen towels in the bath, eggs in a soup can,
She knows everything has teeth and the teeth can bite her,
She knows the cat thinks at her and eats plants to spite her.
She rolls up her mind in a mat and tucks the ends in.
In the past, there were two categories: Being and Thing.

MOAT

Let's solve everything right this minute
While we are all good angry and drunk
Let's not set booze aside for a minute
Down the gullet pour guzzle repeat
Let's have words as they come to us naked
Fresh sizzling hot fritters of hell
Down the fortress wall oil runs boiling
Fleas breed under the collar like fleas
Let's not for a minute stop talking
Words snowballs with pebbles inside
Keep them flying across the green moat now
The last pebble will win the war
Reacting reacting reacting
Cigarette after cigarette cigarette
Important important important
Understand think and feel mean the same

FIBONACCI

The love of a gardening man keeps steady as made.
Whether it's stuffy or drafty, it sits there earthen.
Fibonacci seashells of clay fan out under his spade.
Seed packets are planted in time for unfrivolous birthing.

When your words were coming up frogs in a frying pan,
When your fire was coming up loins and its tongues were hissing,
When the drama confetti would have killed a lighter man,
Trust me – the Claymation man did not even listen.

CRAZY BUS BLUES

I saw you and faltered
I saw you and fell
My plans were altered
I started to tell you
But you never listen
And they always listen, they always listen
They listen to us
But I'm smarter
I ain't going on the crazy bus

I saw you in streets
I saw you in stores
Recurring dreams
Revolving doors
Your countless perfections
In countless windows I saw your reflections
They were all fake
Don't I know it
I ain't going on the crazy bus

Please talk to me
Please let me know
Please talk to me
Or please let me go
I'll make better choices
I'll make better effort to silence the voices
Shut up you voices
Look ma no voices
I ain't going on the crazy bus

MIDDLE ROAD

He asked, "Why the lab coat, you say? We wear them deliberately.
We do client assessments,
I mean, client surveys, in all our stores.
It turns out lab coats impress them.
Especially the hysteroids.
We'll begin by suppressing vitality considerably.
I mean, yours.
We have pharmaceuticals.
It's a secret formula, but in part they're just good old steroids.

Your vitality will be, as we say, down for declension, his up for ascension,
Until there's a middle road that we can discern.
Otherwise, you two won't experience mutual comprehension.
Side effects? Well, constant heartburn. Your stomach will burn.

To treat it, sodium bicarbonate is the only thing you can take.
You'll keep forgetting words, tasks, eating candy right with the wrappers.
But that won't last forever. It's only three months, give or take.
We are not gods, you see. We are just guessers, plodders, scrappers.

Our success, to be honest, is part science, part chance, and
There is a small part of what we might call quantum magic.
People always talked to the dead; it's just that the dead never answered.
People searched for the Water of Life, but it's not even fully a substance,
and definitely nothing pelagic.

How do I explain it? Let's say you buy yarn for knitting,
Just a skein (I always think it's pronounced *skin*)
And you find that the yarn is rather loosely sitting
Inside that paper tube it comes in.

It's hard to knit when it's loose. Tear off the paper wrap,
Smoosh it, wind the yarn on, so it gets more tightly wound.
Now, we have us a hard ball of yarn with smoother nap,
With the paper inside, and the wrap being yarn all around.

That's a loose description. Honestly? Don't be so horrified.
Yes, you want to understand, yes, we all want to know what the plan is,
Yet, you don't seem perturbed that your living world has been greatly de-thingyfied,
With no paper postage, cuckoo clocks, LPs or those guys who tune pianos.

Yes, concerns exist, but they shouldn't seem so weighty.
Yes, right now your prospects may look a little squalid,
But think! Even folks who change their views in a full one-eighty
Inside appear to themselves uninterrupted and solid.

But let's return to your conversation partner, now a new cadaver.
Keep it in mind that, to life, he'll be merely a neighbor.
As a being, at this point, he will be largely a cavern,
His existence, as such, a feat of unspeakable labor.

His ability to talk will depend on the levels of fuel.
Most things they say in a dialogue, alas, are social cliches.
It's true even for those couples whose live dancing used to be so sharply dual
That the bystanders thought it polite to avert their gaze.

If you are serious about this, we'll let you see one sample before committing."
He took me out in the hallway and lead me across and through,
Then gave me a small Bluetooth earbud for transmitting,
And opened a door in the wall, small like a door for a clock cuckoo.

In the oculus, an old grey-haired man loudly asked his addressee,
"How are you? Are you frightened? I need to know! Are you in pain?"
Ramrod-straight in her seat, a dead woman with the face of Empress Dowager Cixi
Synthesized her reply: "It's warm. We're in for some rain."

He said: "They have real trouble forming verbs, as a rule.
But for many, even such conversations prove invaluable.
We're in big demand now, so, for our seances, we rent school after school.
The classrooms are set up just right, and the schools stand empty, so they are available."

One more time, I looked at the scene through that small magnifier,
I saw those two sitting, divided by their middle road, each in a separate bay,
I remembered my own gaping hole, my own desert on fire,
And I said: "Okay, I will try this. How do I pay?"

QUARTZ

She loved him and she wrote him a poem after poem,
An ovum after ovum at nobody's request,
And he will never read them, and he will never know them,
A father missing living children born after his death.

And I don't want to know them, and I don't want to keep them,
And I don't want to hold them, the whole unwieldy sheaf:
Intolerable thoughts of the important people,
That stubborn and unyielding another person's grief.

Her face a prairie compass, a yellow light galactic,
A spotlight now and then on men, then women, also men,
She's bartering on trauma as a strategy and tactic,
She's looking for the one who'll make her hair grow black again.

She wrote a stupid sonnet, she wrote a little dumb thing,
She flung a little tidbit, she sprung a little leak
About her spreading sex crumbs along the beach or something,
And him a hungry seagull with an open yellow beak.

I cannot walk unconscious, and I cannot unsee them
Cast on the beach and swept under the grainy sand that hoards
Inoperable thoughts of the important people,
Those stubborn and unyielding little yellow glints of quartz.

BEACH BOYS

I sit on the sand
And my feet are cold
So I spin them around
There's a thing you don't know
I spin my feet
And a thing comes out
It's a thing you don't know
I put you in your spot
I'm a little red bug
You don't know what I got

I see many rocks
Many rocks are quartz
There's a thing you don't know
Many rocks have smarts
There's a thing you don't know
Many rocks play drums
There's a thing you don't know
Many rocks are dumb
I'm a little blue rock
Dum-dee-dum-dee-dee-dum

MARKED DISHEVELED IN CLASS

Data bran scrapes the digestive chute of my brain without ever becoming knowledge, these days.
I just read about Eugene Debs.
Hell if I know what I just read.
Picking a book to bring on the plane,
I had to ask my daughter if I'd read Virgin Suicides.
You read it, Mom.
Thank-you-dear.
My hair was bugging me yesterday: too long.
I put my hands in the back of my head and they, by themselves, executed a basket-o-braids.
Skills unused since Grade 4: full command.
We were not allowed to wear our hair down in elementary school.
We were upbraided.
Another yesterday, my daughter asked me about embroidery.
Propelled by invisible machinery, a cuckoo came out of the door of my mouth.
Molineux thread,
Tambour stitch,
Wrong needle,
Loop here,
Push there,
Knot here,
Hide that.
I have not embroidered anything in thirty years: full command.
The fences are pasted over with old person fallacies.
In My Day, they taught us Real Knowledge.
These Days, they teach Fake Knowledge.
That is why I Knew Things before!
In My Day, they put things in My Brain.
Ergo, either this is Not My Day, or Not My Brain.

KETTLE

Things will precipitate. You've been a little slovenly, so stay at home, put headphones on, then put the kettle on. In this Bermuda state – the sink, the fridge, the oven – you must do the dishes, stand the rain and keep the curtains drawn.

In this Bermuda triangle you watch the waters swollen with carcasses of warriors of every stripe and knack; you sit and watch the struggle between the kettle calling, between the kettle calling and the pot that's clapping back.

These rivers not of Babylon but Babel, waters falling, your waterfalls in headphones, water boiling down below – Herr Falco! Help me, help me, Schatz! Is this the kettle calling? Is this the keh-keh-kettle, hello, hello, hello?

Lest the exposure render your tender self cirrhotic, stay home and let the kettle whistle; then, you tilt and pour, and with a heckle hectic, and with a rattle rhotic the clatter of opinion will roll under the floor.

COUNT OUT

Whenever I've had quite a day
I go to my old bed
I think of those who like me
And I name them in my head
Well Jack likes me for helping
And John likes me for sex
And Jill likes me for venting to
About her noxious ex
Jane likes that I'm her in-group
Despite that see below
Joan likes I'm not her out-group
How little does she know
And Jimmy likes my poems
Which he thinks are about him
And Jerry doesn't like them
'Cause he thinks they're about Jim
And Joe likes me remotely
As his wife is not remote
I fit completely totally
Inside his mental tote
And so I do my mental calculations due to that
I need a human rental in which to hang my hat

MAIN AND BROAD

I have a plan
To live in a place
With a pointless name
Like Ortonville
Uneven streets
A drainage ditch
Hortonville
Mortonville
Nortonville
If I'm ever torn
Like a skin tag
Off serving orifices
And surfaces
A nondescript ranch
A nameless hag
Fifty dollars a week
Worth of groceries
I have a plan
To live in a place
Of progress and culture barren
If any neighbors
Come chat me up
I'll tell them my name is Karen
I would go to anyone's
Methodist church
November wind as a fetter
I would be a no-one
Just like myself
Honestville it doesn't matter

BEAUREGARD

I have no self-esteem.
I don't have any self-esteem in the same way I don't have a cow.
I don't use a cow.
I do have something, but it is far from a cow.
More like a little-known and oft-forgotten squirrel.
One may ask, what are you?
And I may fling my hair off my face and say plummily,
Colin Edward Michael Blunstone.
I can put on all my temporary gold tattoos at once, and it won't mean a thing.
So maybe from the outside this biopic looks like a melodrama with Jennifer Jason Leigh.
I'd rather watch it as a sketch show with Viggo Mortensen.
It is not indicative of me losing my mind.
It is indicative of me having my mind.
I'm always it, and it never matters a whit.

FLAVOR OF THE DAY

So, you're here for a new day today. What flavor packet?
Still groggy from sleep, I said: I don't know what flavor. Just hit me.
She flipped a switch. The machine whirred with a steady contented racket.
She took my vitals, then threw them away and began to fit me.

She said: sorry 'bout that, but it's still the procedure to take the vitals.
We need to make sure you have them, but it doesn't matter if they are faster or calmer.
Also – sorry, today we are all out of hazelnut and a few other vials.
Now, how much time would you say you like to devote to thinking about Laura Palmer?

Let me write your name on the cup. Brian? I feel like I know you already.
So, this base rides in hard: first, you're very involved with your kids, and then not at all.
Short term, a person or object will get lost; it's a new add-in called Drop in the Eddy.
We trial it on mature customers instead of the older, bolder Waterfall.

And kids these days, they digivape their flavors. It's a slightly different experience.
Corporate develops new add-ins for them at a very productive rate.
Back to Laura Palmer! You seem to take your film reviewing seriously,
So, I'll add True to Type, to guarantee you a solid two hours of fruitless online debate.

Well, I'm nearly done. Just let me add a little Insult to Injury.
Oh, come on, now. You know them rules! It's one free to go, and one down.
I'll just sprinkle in something seasonal, pumpkiny, gingery,
And a complimentary shot of a clear singing cherry at sundown.

Enjoy your day, Brian!

MAGYCK

Black radish, raw honey, badger fat, mustard water.
Magic gives you tools.
Science takes away the tools and makes the world loom over you in naked dominion.
An old Russian woman goes to the doctor and is comforted by his words for what ails her.
Ischemia.
Spondylitis.
She carries the words in her mouth like water to other old women.
What you've named, you've caught, you've cornered, you've conquered.
Latin is for incantations.
Take a small white pill at sunrise and a small yellow pill before bed: a remedy.
A remedy remedies.
The baba is satisfied.
This is the magic of the medicine man.
The science of the medicine man says autoimmune.
Incurable, degenerative, dead cells, dead ends.
Science agitates the old woman.
What do you mean, incurable? Why are you here, medicine man? What good are you?
Three times a day with my meals I take these, three times, and I say three Ar-Fathers, and I apply the juice of black radish mixed with honey to my chest.
Heal me, Saint Prednisone.
Don't talk to me of superstition, science, faith, facts, you thirty-year-old nothing!
You are not hurting yet.
You don't know from facts.

A BROKEN VAUDEVILLE

Who 'twixt us hasn't had an awful day?
Who hasn't turned for comfort to a lie?
Who hasn't lost a needle in the hay?

Who hasn't lost a needle in the hay?
Who hasn't had a big unstopping cry?
Who hasn't looked for a swain in the hay?

Who hasn't rolled a pearl before a swine?
Who hasn't robbed a Peter to pay Paul?
Who hasn't rolled a roach, a die, an eye?

Who hasn't bought saltpeter for a price?
Who hasn't popped a Peter to pay Rob?
Who hasn't Dark and Stormy Rob and Roy?

Who hasn't rubbed saltpeter on her wounds?
Whose eyes did rhyme but did not rhyme with sounds?
Who hasn't traded pepper to salt snow?
Whose sugar didn't melt in salty rain?

Who hasn't called a Saul to borrow salt?
Who hasn't been a Paul becoming Saul?
Who hasn't been brought down from warm to sad?
Who hasn't peeled dishonor off herself?
Who hasn't been a villain to a saint?
Who hasn't danced a broken villanelle?

MORMOIRE

I'm ready to wrap
The miseries of the day
In a large leaf
I can't hold them anymore

I'm having a bad day
And I've already had one before
And one before
Before

I'm not allowed to leave
I'm held in position by witnesses
The children
The old
Pegs

The children are baking miseries in them
Miseries in new leaves
Larvae of miseries
Eggs

WHAT WE HAVE TRIED

Bloodletting
Leeches
Brushing the beaches
Being the best
Inspirational speeches
Just being honest
Reading the signs
Sandwiches
Which
Have crossed
State lines
Stalemates
Aspirin
Cardiac aspirin
Tincture of larkspur
Spirit whispering
Spitting
Splitting
Vodka with Sprite
I think we better call it a night

FRIDGE

An hour of free time, and I cleaned the fridge, I cleaned the fridge.

Had a bottle of Sam Adams Cherry Wheat, the new definition of uneventful, and so am I, and so is me.

An opened can of red kidney beans and a glass jar of grape jelly slid off the wonky shelf and torpedoed the floor, but I caught the hoisin sauce mid-flight, and I caught the shelf, I rescued the sheet of glass, the new definition of uneventful, and so am I, and so is me.

Listened to the suggested Summer Hits Playlist, Otis Redding, Grateful Dead, the new definition of uneventful, and so is me.

Then the three men I admire the most caught the last train for the coast, and the fridge is done, the fridge is done, I will have some soup, or another Cherry Wheat, or both.

SUNDIAL

Suddenly I was sleeping in the sun
The sundial spun, I started feeling sick
My son was sawing plywood by the stack
The sticking of the nails went six-eight-ten

A sharp steel tray flew through the plate of glass
It fell down shuddering and then lay still
The shards went studding space but none have struck
Hospital art of harvest gold and mauve

I said, when can I have my deathrow steak
You said, endure, you'll be an ataman
And then I knew that it did not work out
I wasn't leaving hospital that day

I would not be a batman and my son
Would not return the nails to my weak hands
They said, your kids have come all stuffed with words
Right, the catwoman doctor lied again

Just so I wouldn't fret and yank my shirt
Small suns were sliding on the ceiling white
Small needles bristled up my scaly skin
My eyes were sealing on a sliding scale

TIMEFRAME

Here's a man who is trying to avoid rain
He tries to take matter into his own hands
Graphite makes and fills his black outline
He leaps around streetlights to outrun the winds

Here's a woman whose breasts have lost their charge
They are sacks of meat, titties suggested for sissies
Her outline sags and her black sine waves surge
At irregular clicks as she strobes up with red losses

Their frames keep clicking through all the time clocked
By all the clocks eaten by Big Muzzy
Thank you for opening this envelope that I licked
I know you are very busy

RIDDLE

Jenny, Jenny with a frown,
Who may turn you upside down,
For a day or for a sigh?
None that may and some that try.

Jenny, Jenny with a pout,
Who may turn you inside out,
For a sigh or for a day?
None that try and some that may.

www.ingramcontent.com/pod-product-compliance
Lightning Source LLC
Chambersburg PA
CBHW022120090426
42743CB00008B/929